The Zebra Outdoor Book

Whether you live in the country or the town there is always plenty to do out of doors. You can find out more about the town or village you live in, learn how to make model boats and planes, or grow your own garden or window box.

This is a book full of suggestions for these and many other ideas to start you off on an absorbing hobby or help you spend a free afternoon.

Cover illustration by Desmond Clover

Published by Evans Brothers Limited
Montague House, Russell Square,
London, W.C.1.

© Evans Brothers Limited 1971

First published 1971

Set in 12 on 14 point Baskerville
Printed in Great Britain
by Cox & Wyman Ltd.,
London, Reading and Fakenham

CSD 237 35214 1   PR 1884
PB 237 35212 5

Contents

Read this first

Have you ever dreamed of becoming an explorer and having exciting journeys through jungles and across deserts in search of strange animals and distant cities? Well you may never cross any deserts but there is nothing to stop you from becoming an explorer. An explorer is simply a person who is interested enough to find out about things, and it does not mean that you have to travel very far. All around us are exciting and interesting things to explore and find out about.

Some of this exploring can be done indoors but in this book we are going to be concerned with those things that are outdoor activities. Most of them require nothing more than curiosity and a pair of sharp eyes, some require skill and patience, but all of them can be done by anybody, almost anywhere and at any time.

Before we look at some of these ideas in detail, there are one or two points which apply to most of them. Before you make a start in any of these activities take a while to think about them; to decide what you are hoping to do; check over what you will need as many a good outing has been spoilt because something had been forgotten or left at home.

For many of the hobbies it will help if you can make notes and it is a good idea to make yourself a clip board. Take a piece of hardboard, plywood or even thick cardboard, which is just a bit bigger than the paper you plan to use. Now take a good bull-dog or spring clip and slip this over one end, and use it to hold the paper firmly in place on the board. Often it is more convenient to use a ball-point pen or fibre-tipped pen rather than a pencil for then you won't be held up by broken points. However, before you start out check that the pens are not nearly empty and likely to run out just when you need them.

Many of the activities dealt with in this book will produce more interesting results if you can persuade friends to join in so that you can pool your results and, in any case, most things are more fun if you can share them.

Not all the ideas in this book are concerned with exploring and many sections are intended to give you ideas of how you can tackle some slightly unusual hobby.

One final piece of advice; whenever you set out to try something a little bit difficult, especially if it involves any risks, take care and don't do anything silly. *If you are going any distance let your parents or friends know where you are likely to be and how long you will be away.* Even the best and bravest explorers take care and do their best to avoid accidents.

After each section there is a list of books which will help you to find out more about each topic. Most of them you will be able to find in the public library but some of the cheaper ones you may like to buy for yourselves. You will find included in most of the lists some 'discovering' books, published by Shire Publications, Tring, Herts, and these cost only a few shillings and are obtainable from bookshops. Another useful series are the 'I Spy' books published by the Dickens Press, 4, Upper Thames Street, London E.C.4, which you can buy in bookshops and many newsagents.

Many of the outdoor activities mentioned in this book will mean that you have to travel on foot, on your bicycle or in your parent's car. To ensure that you travel in safety at all times get hold of a copy of the 'Highway Code'. This little book tells you all about the signals that motorists use and the safe way to use the roads whether you are a pedestrian or a motorist. Ten minutes spent reading this little booklet could well prove invaluable.

Getting About

Walking

Because we do it nearly every day of our lives few of us think of walking as a pastime but it can be one of the cheapest, easiest and most enjoyable of all. You need little special equipment and it is a pastime that can be carried out in town or country.

Wherever you walk there are a few things to remember. As you will depend on your feet it is as well to pay special attention to them and probably the most important point of all is to have well-fitting, strong shoes. Slippers may be light and comfortable but they are not very good for walking on pavements or scrambling along stony paths. Never wear new shoes if you are planning to walk any long distance for all new footwear is a little stiff and tight and needs to be 'broken in'.

Blisters are painful and take all the fun out of walking so avoid them by wearing good socks and well-fitting shoes. Before you start out sprinkle your feet with talcum powder. A small tin of adhesive plasters is something that you should have in your pocket so that if you are unlucky enough to get a blister you can cover it and make sure that it gets rubbed as little as possible.

For walking in town there are probably no other arrangements or equipment needed, but if you plan to walk in the open country there are one or two other things that you will need. A walking stick or short staff can be very useful for parting bushes, testing the depth of pools or puddles as well as being jolly handy for helping you along.

If your journey is going to take you away from roads and paths and across country then you really need a compass and a map. Before you start out look at the map and make sure that you know what the various symbols on it stand for. The size of the map will obviously depend on how far you propose to walk but the bigger the scale the better, for this means that the map can tell you more. It is a very good idea to get hold of a plastic envelope or bag to use as a case to protect the folded map from the rain. Talking of rain, don't forget to take a raincoat with you; modern lightweight plastic mackintoshes take up little room and weigh so litttle. Don't choose too thin a mackintosh for in open country the wind could cause it to flap about so that it would give little protection.

If you plan to be out for long don't forget that you will most certainly want to eat and that means taking some food, but choose carefully and pick things, like cheese, that are light and take up little space. For all these extra bits and pieces you will require some sort of carrier and the most popular for walking are called rucksacks and fit over the shoulders and hang down the back, leaving your arms and hands free. They are very comfortable if they fit properly so make sure that yours does or else you will very soon have a sore back and aching shoulders.

Perhaps you are asking yourself why you should walk when it is so much easier and quicker by car? Well that is part of the reason, for these days we all tend to rush about in cars, planes and trains and pass things by so quickly we have no time to look at them properly. Stroll along a road or across the country and you will be most surprised at the things you see. After you have looked through the section on EXPLORING you will probably find many things to look out for and walking will undoubtedly be the best way to find them.

Useful books
Use your legs, Guy R. Williams. (Chapman and Hall.)

Cycling

If you want to travel further and faster than by foot then the simplest means is to cycle. Not so long ago nearly everybody could and did ride a bicycle but now, except for a few special towns like Oxford, few people bother to use bicycles. In countries like Holland they are still as popular as ever and thousands of people cycle to work.

Today's traffic has made all roads dangerous for everybody so the golden rule is: *take care all the time*.

Remember that as a cyclist you can alter direction, swerve, or stop quicker than any other vehicle on the road so always give plenty of warning of what you are going to do by means of clear and careful hand signals. Before you take out your bicycle always look it over and make sure that it is in good condition and safe to ride. Check that all the nuts and bolts are tight; test your brakes and see that they are correctly adjusted and not worn; see that the chain is neither too tight nor too slack. Make sure that the saddle and handlebars are at the correct height so that when you are sitting on the saddle your feet can touch the ground without strain.

Before you do any real cycling why not take the Cycling Proficiency Test? The training for this test will teach you how to look after your cycle; how to ride carefully and safely as well as making sure you know the Highway Code. If you pass the test you are awarded a badge and a certificate but, far more important, you will be a better cyclist than when you started. If you do not know where to take the test ask your teacher, the local police station, or at the Public Library.

Cycling is always good exercise and also has the advantage that you can get along roads and lanes impassable to almost every other kind of vehicle. If you do come to a really difficult place you can always pick up your bicycle and carry it safely past and then remount and ride on.

As with walking, before you start out on your cycling tour always check over your equipment which you can probably best carry in a bag attached to the back of the saddle. Make sure that you have your compass, maps, tools, pump and puncture outfit. It is as well to keep a cape, or plastic mackintosh permanently in the saddle bag, then you will never be caught unprepared.

When you are a little older you may well like to join a cycling club that will organise tours, rallies, scrambles and races. If you become keen on any of these activities you will probably want special equipment and this can make cycling a more expensive hobby.

Like any true explorer plan your route before you start your ride. Try to choose interesting routes and ones that avoid, as far as possible, busy main roads. If you plan to visit one special place check on the map and see if you can choose a route that will incorporate one or two other sights as well so that you can get a maximum return for all your effort. When planning your route don't forget to allow time for short stops, time to eat, and so on and if you are likely to be out late make certain that your lights are all in working order.

Finally, remember to let somebody in the family know exactly where you plan to go and how long you expect to be. This will help to prevent anybody worrying about you whilst you are out.

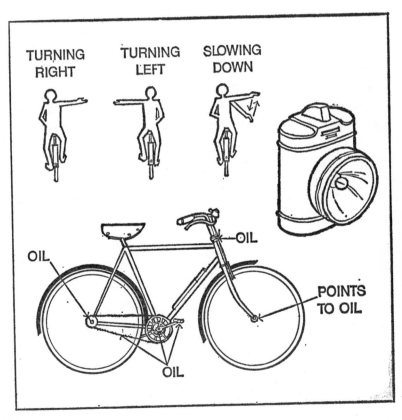

If you use your bicycle very much then every so often do a major overhaul and give an extra check. Remember that dirt and damp will produce rust and may damage the cycle's paintwork, so give the frame and rims of the wheel a good wipe over. Carry out a double check on all the nuts and bolts and ensure that all the items in your saddle bag are present and correct. Finally oil all moving parts such as the hubs of the wheel, the chain and base of the handlebars. These regular checks will keep your cycle looking better, running better and reduce the chances of a breakdown or accident.

Useful Books
Cycling Manual, R. John Way. (Temple Books.)
Cycling Handbook, A. L. Pullen. (Pitman.)
Cycling for You, Ronald English. (Lutterworth Press.)

Collecting

Car Numbers

When you travel or just walk around have you ever looked at the hundreds of cars that pass you by? There are so many makes differing in colour, size and shape and design but they all have one thing in common, a registration or index mark. Only the Queen is allowed to own a car without a registration plate. These plates are displayed on the front and back of the car, usually just below the front bumper and above the rear bumper. The plate is made up of two main parts – letters and numbers – and it is rather like a car's birth certificate for it can tell you where, and often when, the car was first registered.

The more interesting part of the index are the letters for they give the place of registration. Authorities throughout the country are given sets of letters which they issue to all cars registered with them, for example those registered in Chester have the letters FM, those from Orkney BS, those from Glamorgan L. The numbers following the letters belong to the particular car carrying them and are used by it as long as it is in existence.

Some plates have a group of letters, usually up to three in number, then the number followed by a single letter, e.g. GK 607 A. This last letter tells you the year in which the car was registered – in this example 1963.

Cars imported into England are given letter groups beginning with Q.

A full list of the Index marks is given in the A.A. Handbook and you can probably get one of these from your parents or a friend who has a car. There is also a smaller list in *The Zebra Book of Facts for Boys*.

A few letter combinations you will not find in the list and these are special ones which are held by people who like to have their own personal identification.

If you decide that it is an interesting idea to collect car numbers, it is so easy to start for all you need is a clipboard or notebook, a ball-point pen and a safe place by the side of the road. Obviously the busier the road the more numbers you can collect in a short time but it is also the kind of collecting that you can do at any time – on the way to school or sitting at your front window.

Since the number of cars is likely to be fairly high you probably won't have time to check each one at the time that you see it, so it is probably best simply to record them at the time and identify them at home.

There are many different ways of collecting these numbers. You can collect as many as possible and go in for quantity, or you can make it more difficult by looking out for certain counties or towns. Another variation is to try for a group of cars all from one authority perhaps a Ford, an Austin and a Rover all registered in London. This kind of collecting is specially interesting if you are travelling around the country for you obviously stand a better chance of getting a variety of registrations.

There is another kind of plate that you will find on a car and this is a small, oval one, usually mounted on the front and back. These are international plates which give the country of origin of the car — G.B. for British cars travelling abroad.

D for Germany. If you ever see one bearing the letters SU, that is a rare one for it means the car was registered in Russia.

A variation on the 'car number' game is to ignore the letters and watch for the numbers which have to be collected in strict order. To start you have to see a car bearing just the number 1 on its plate, then you start looking for 2 and so on. You can either set a top limit and see how soon you get to 50 or you can go on for as long as you like. No doubt, you can think of variations such as a race between a group of your friends.

Useful Books
The Zebra Book of Facts for Boys, Cyril Parsons. (Evans.)

Fossils

Millions of years ago, long before man appeared, tiny creatures, rather like snails, lived on earth. They died and their bodies fell on the ground or into the sea. Deposits of mud and earth drifted over to cover them. As the years passed the bodies and deposits were gradually crushed and changed into a solid rock-like material. Today these rock-like remains may still be found and the search for fossils, for that is what they are called, is an exciting one.

Unfortunately fossils have only survived in certain kinds of rock and it is useless to look for them except where you find these rocks. Rocks which were thrust up from below the earth's crust were far too hot for any life to exist on them. The best areas for fossil hunting are those where there are soft rocks, known as sedimentary rocks, such as limestone, chalk or a flake-like type known as shale.

You therefore need to know where you can find these rocks and to do this you must look at a map of your area which shows the types of rocks – these are called geological maps. Your school or public library is very likely to have copies.

If you are near an area where these rocks are to be found

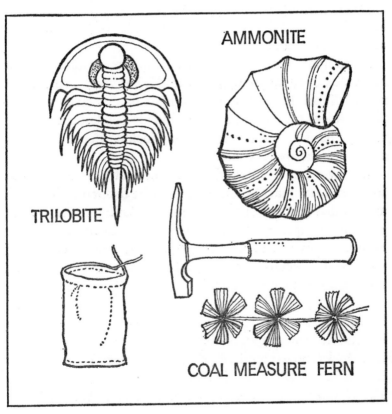

AMMONITE

TRILOBITE

COAL MEASURE FERN

then you are lucky and can start your hunt. It will not be easy to find fossils and it means careful looking. A good pointer is to watch for 'layers' in the rocks and concentrate your search on the point where such layers meet. You can often spot the layers by the differences in colour and texture of the rocks. It is possible you may find a piece of bone from a terrible lizard, a dinosaur, or a tooth of a mammoth, but it is far more likely that you will find a small creature, rather like a snail – an ammonite. Another type looks rather like a lady-bird with legs sticking out all around it – a trilobite; both these fossils are fairly common.

Fossil hunting needs little special equipment apart from a haversack to carry your finds in and a hammer. You can get special 'fossil' hammers but any light hammer can be used just to knock off the soft rock. An old kitchen knife is a useful tool for hacking out any interesting looking items, for chalk and limestone are very soft.

One word of warning. Some of the best hunting grounds for fossils are quarries and these can be dangerous for some are flooded and in others there may be falling rocks. *Do not go into any quarry without asking permission and always take care*. If you are in doubt go along and see the curator of your local museum who will probably be able to advise you about the best places to look.

Useful Books
Fossils, H. Swinnerton. (Collins.)
Our Rocks and Minerals, A. White. (Ladybird.)
British Fossils, D. Forbes. (A. & C. Black.)
Tales Told by Fossils, C. L. Fenton. (World's Work.)

Leaves and Plants

As winter ends and spring begins to take over, go for a stroll around your garden, the park, the common or the countryside. Look at the plants beginning to come to life again with their delicate leaves and buds – they are things of beauty and worthy of close examination and you might like to collect some of them.

Remember that these are growing, living things and take only what you really need for your collection, never pull off the leaves or buds haphazardly for you could well kill off the plant or at least prevent its blossoming.

You will need something in which to carry home your specimens and since they are rather delicate it is important to take care that they are not damaged. A small tin or plastic box containing some kitchen tissues will prevent the specimens jolting about and perhaps breaking. In the case of small wild flowers you may want to take home a complete plant and it is as well to have something with which you can dig out the root – a trowel, small spade or old tablespoon. Don't forget to record where and when you found each specimen and if you cannot identify it at once mark it with a number so that there will be no confusion between specimen and details.

What should you collect? Well you can tackle it several ways. The simplest is to collect a sample of any plant that you come across and in this fashion you can soon build up a fair-sized display of local plants. Another approach is to concentrate on a few examples and aim at getting a display showing the growth pattern by mounting a series of plants in different stages of development – rather like an album.

Another way is to concentrate your search on one particular field, patch of garden, or bank and collect one example of every plant and grass growing within that area. If you make a sketch map of the area and mark on it where you find each type of plant, you may well find some kind of pattern for certain plants prefer certain kinds of soil or situation.

Once you have gathered your specimens they must be prepared for display by pressing and drying them. Clean off any dirt and earth and decide whether you want to use all the plant or just a leaf or so. A careful rinse with cold water will probably be sufficient. Once the specimen is clean it must be pressed and this can be done quite simply without any special equipment.

Take the plant, as fresh as possible for best results, and place it on a sheet of blotting paper which is resting on several sheets of newspaper. Arrange the leaves, stalk and flower in the position you want and cover the plant with another sheet of blotting paper and more newspaper. On top of this pile place a piece of hardboard or plywood and on this place some weights – books are quite suitable – and leave it for several days. Then check the plant and change the damp blotting paper to prevent it from going mouldy. Using newspaper will also speed up the drying. Leave the plant long enough to make sure that it is thoroughly dry.

If you plan to collect a large number of plants it is probably worth while making yourself a cheap and simple press. Find two boards, preferably the same size, and on both of them drill a hole near each corner. Buy four bolts with butterfly nuts and eight large washers; pass each bolt through one washer and then up through both boards and place a washer over the top projecting end. Then put on the butterfly nut and the press is ready. When you prepare a drying pad it can be slipped between the boards which are then screwed up tight.

Once the plant is thoroughly dried and pressed it can be mounted for display in a variety of ways. The two most common methods are to mount them in large albums, or to

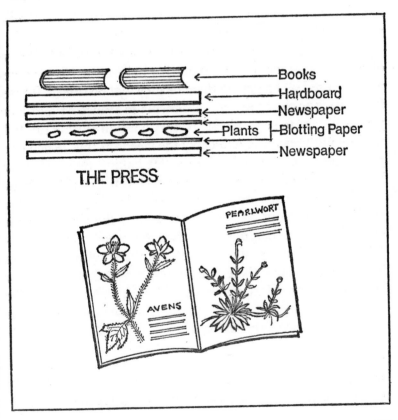

THE PRESS

mount them on separate sheets of card or paper. Secure the plants to the backing by narrow strips of transparent, sticky tape, or by an adhesive applied directly to the plant. Beneath each item note the main details such as name, type and where collected. You will need reference books to do this job properly and you can probably get all you want from the library although many are very cheap and you may like to buy them yourself. Note the scientific name as well as the popular name – *umbelliferae* sounds much more impressive than hogweed but they are the same plant.

A similar procedure is used for the preparation and display of seaweeds although there is one big difference. No pressure must be used when drying them or they will be ruined. These fascinating growths are more difficult to transport and it is probably best to use a plastic box with a tight-fitting lid. Fill the box with seawater and carry the weeds in this. When you get home pour the water into a flat baking tin or shallow baking tray and then float the seaweed in the water. Now slide a piece of card into the tray under the seaweed and very carefully lift it out on the card; arrange the plant to your satisfaction and then place the card and weed on top of several sheets of newspaper. Cover the weed with a piece of butter muslin and then some more newspaper. And now leave it to dry. Most seaweeds will stick themselves to the card as they dry but if they do not, then secure them in the same way as leaves and flowers.

Useful Books
'*I Spy*' *Books* (Dickens Press).
Wild Flowers; Wild Fruits and Fungi; Garden Flowers.

Exploring the Park, Leslie Jackman. (Evans.)
Exploring the Hedgerow, Leslie Jackman. (Evans.)
Exploring the Seashore, Leslie Jackman. (Evans.)
Exploring the Woodland, Leslie Jackman. (Evans.)
Ladybird Books
British Wild Flowers, B. Vesey-Fitzgerald.
Garden Flowers, B. Vesey-Fitzgerald.
'Discovering' Books (Shire Press).
The Folklore of Plants; English Gardens.

Traffic

We suffer from too much traffic today and its noise, damage
and danger are a menace to us, but since we all use the cars
and lorries we are all responsible. However, have you ever
really looked at the traffic? What type of vehicle is most
common in your area? Which is the most popular car? Which
is the busiest time of the day? Well, you can discover the
answers to all these questions. You will probably find it simpler if you take a friend along with you for it is so much easier
to keep count if you split the job and work together.

Choose a fine day and then, equipped with your clip board
and writing materials, take up a nice safe place by the road-
side. Before you start out it will probably save time and
trouble if you prepare some sheets. The way you set out the
sheets will depend on what you are aiming to do. If you are
interested in the various makes of car you could divide your
sheet into columns headed FORD, MORRIS, JAGUAR, etc. If it is
the type of vehicle that concerns you then the headings could

be VANS, CARS, LORRIES, CYCLES, etc. As each vehicle passes a certain point you place a tick in the appropriate column. If the traffic is heavy then don't bother to count ticks but leave this job for a more leisurely moment. One convenient way is to cross through each block of ten.

The information is not very interesting if you leave it as a mass of ticks or crosses so when you have done your count you

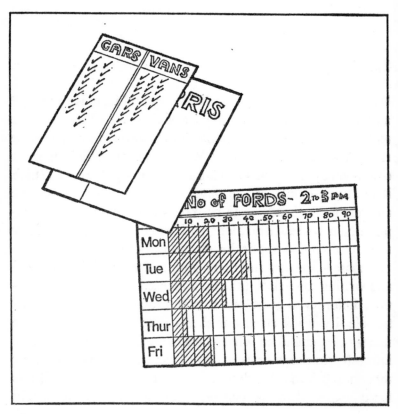

can display the totals in the form of block graphs or histograms. Again it will also make a very interesting comparison if you do several counts at the same place but at different times of the day. Another alternative is to carry out counts at set times on different days of the week.

After a few counts you will find that you have learnt a tremendous amount about the traffic of your town or village.

Useful Books
'*I Spy*' *Books* (Dickens Press).
Cars; Road Transport; Motor Cycles and Cycles; Sports Cars.
Ladybird Books
The Motor Car, D. Carey.
The Story of the Motor Car, D. Carey.
Motor Cars, D. Carey.
Commercial Vehicles, D. Carey.

Trains

If you live near a railway line or near a large station you may well take little or no notice of the trains but they make quite an interesting study. There are still one or two steam trains running on private lines and these are colourful and exciting, but even the more common diesel is of interest. All locomotives, like cars, have a number and many people find a great deal of fun and interest in listing the numbers of trains that pass them. Some mainline stations have special arrangements for enthusiasts to have places on the platforms where they can stand out of harm's way and record the numbers of the trains. If you are lucky enough to be near a station you can check with the station master if there are any such arrangements.

Apart from recording locomotive numbers you might like to look at the various types of rolling stock that passes you, for

there are so many special types of trucks and carriages designed for special purposes.

If you have any interest in the railways then you may well like to visit the Railway Museum at York or the Transport Museum in London. For collectors there is the British Railway Shop in London which specialises in selling surplus items of historical interest.

Useful Books
Railways, Eric Baxter. (Bodley Head.)
'*I Spy*' *Books* (Dickens Press).
A Train Journey.
Ladybird Books
How it Works – The Locomotive, D. Carey.
The Story of Railways, R. Bowood.

Exploring

Your Town or Village

We all get so used to the everyday scene that soon we hardly notice it until one day a shop changes, a building is demolished or a new one erected and we find it hard to remember what was there before the change. Instead of walking past without looking, why not start exploring the place where you live? If you do, it is fairly certain that you will be surprised at some of the things that you never noticed before. Even if you live in one of the new towns there is still a great deal of interesting material that you can discover in your neighbourhood.

There is history and interest in almost everything about you. Take a stroll along the main street in your town – have you ever wondered why it should be that particular shape? If your town is not very old it is probably a fairly straight road but if the town is of any age the road probably bends and there was, at one time, a reason for this. It may be that there once was a footpath here; perhaps the road passed round a pool long since gone, or there may be any one of a dozen explanations. This is just one of the interesting things that you could find out whilst exploring your town, so let's look at some of the everyday things in the street.

Houses

Today most people live in houses or flats but hardly ever spare a glance for the outside of the buildings. Look at the brickwork, especially the arrangement of the bricks for there are different ways of placing them. See how many ways you can spot.

Now look at the house itself – can you see any difference in shape and design between a house built in the last ten years and one built fifty or a hundred years ago? If you can visit a really old town you may well be able to see houses that were built over three hundred years ago and these will probably be of the timber-framed variety and easily recognised by their exposed wooden beams. In the 17th century builders started to use far more bricks and the houses began to look more like present day ones. In the 18th century nearly all houses were of brick and in the town there were an increasing number of houses built together in lines – these are called terraces.

You can spot 18th-century houses by their tall, rectangular shape and the way in which the height of the window decreases towards the top of the house. In the 19th century there was a tremendous increase in the number of people living in towns and to give them somewhere to live large numbers of small houses were built – many of them so crowded together that their backs almost touched one another. If you live in a town like Birmingham, London, Glasgow or Manchester, among others, you are bound to find some of these houses as you wander round. In the late Victorian period more elaborate and decorative houses were built. Often they were quite large with fancy porches and doorways. Early this century a number of houses were built in a style which copied earlier fashions and you may well find some mock-Tudor houses.

Streets

Apart from the houses have you ever thought of looking and thinking about the names of the streets in your town? Have you got a Beaconsfield Road, a Montgomery Square or a Churchill Gardens near you? If so you may not realise that they are all named after famous people. If there is a local character or some national figure connected with your town there may well be streets named after him. Other street names may recall the town or country as it used to be before the streets were built – Orchard Row, Pond Road, Greenwood Street, are all that may remain of the old countryside now completely covered by houses.

Why not take a stroll or cycle ride around your neighbourhood and note down the names of some of the streets and then sit down at leisure and see if you can find their origins? The best places to look are the local museum, if you have one, and the local library, for at these places there will be experts able to advise you.

While you are out exploring the names of the streets spare a glance down at the pavements. You will probably be quite surprised at the number of things set into it. Fire hydrants are recognised by everybody but what about the key-hole shaped metal lids?

If the street is of any age you will be sure to find some

circular metal plates set into the pavement and these are the lids covering a chute leading down to a coal cellar beneath the pavement. When houses were warmed by coal fires stocks of fuel were kept in these cellars and to avoid having the coalman walk through the house coal-chutes were fitted. The coal-chute covers are of cast iron and are often most interesting with patterns and the name of the firm making them in raised letters.

If you find some, instead of drawing them why not take a rubbing? For this job you will need some stout paper, a number of wax crayons or else a ball of wax, and a soft brush. First brush off all pieces of grit or dirt from the cover, then pull over it a large sheet of paper weighted down at the corners with bricks or anything else to hand. Now rub the wax carefully backwards and forwards across the paper, pressing firmly but evenly all the time – not too hard or you will tear the paper, and not too lightly or you will not get a clear impression. Gradually the pattern of the cover will begin to show clearly in white and the colour of the crayon. When you return home you can cut out the shape and mount it on a sheet of thin card or cartridge paper and use it as a decoration, or it can be mounted in a large-sized book. Don't forget to add details of the site of the cover and the date that you did the rubbing.

After you have looked at the pavement look up higher at the walls – but don't forget to watch where you are going! On many of the older houses you may find a plaque fitted to the walls, including some which give the date when the houses were built. On a few houses you may find some metal plates which are likely to be either boundary marks or fire insurance plates. Towns and villages, in the past, were divided into sections known as parishes each of which was the responsibility of a church and the parish took its name from that church. The limits of each parish were indicated by metal plates set into the walls of buildings. These plates usually bear the initials of the church and a date when the boundary was marked.

Fire marks are a relic of the days when there were no public fire brigades but only those organised by insurance companies. When you wanted to insure your house against fire you paid the premium and you were then issued with a metal plate which was fastened to the wall of your house. If there was a fire the insurance engine arrived and if there was a plaque on the wall the firemen tackled the fire. These marks are often made in the shape of the symbol of the company such as a sun, clasped hands (The Hand in Hand Company), or a phoenix.

Another part of old houses always worth looking at are the doorways; many of the door knockers were elaborate and made in the shape of lion's heads, faces or vases of flowers. By the side of the door you may well see torch extinguishers which were rather like metal cornets into which the burning torches were pushed. Look down as well as up and you may be lucky enough to spot a foot-scraper. These were very necessary as the streets were often thick with mud and filth which would have been walked into the house unless there was something on which to scrape the muck off the shoes.

At a time when most people were unable to read, shopkeepers advertised their goods by hanging a sign outside their shops; a locksmith had a key and there was a saw for a tool-maker. There is still one in common use today – the barber's red and white striped pole – do you know why they have this particular sign? Can you find others still used?

As you stroll around look at some of the banks, schools and public houses. Can you see anything that they have in common? Most of these buildings have what is commonly

called a coat-of-arms, which is a 'picture sign' telling people something about the owner. You can find out quite a lot about the coats-of-arms and the art of heraldry from some of the many books on the subject. Parts of the coats-of-arms are often used by public houses as their sign – Red Lion, Green Dragon, White Lion and many others. Here is another sort of collection for as you cycle round you could look out for some of these names and signs. There are many other fascinating things that you can spot – look out for unusual signs, mile-stones, old inns, gateways, statues or any other relic of the past.

You can probably find many exciting places and things to explore but there are two kinds of buildings that you will certainly enjoy visiting, castles and churches.

Castles

The earliest were simply hilltops fortified by ditches and walls of earth – one of the largest is Maiden Castle in Dorset but there are many others dotted about the country.

When the Romans came they built great stone forts and there are several of their castles in Britain. Colchester is one of the best known and there is, of course, their magnificent Hadrian's wall.

When William led his troops to victory at Hastings he needed castles quickly to keep his hold on England and his men built motte and bailey castles. These were simply high earthen hills surrounded by a deep ditch; at the top of the hill, the motte, was a fenced enclosure. The fencing has long since gone but you can still find the hills – there is a very good one at Thetford in Norfolk.

38

Wooden walls were not strong enough to hold off big attacks so they were soon replaced by thick stone walls. At the corners of these stone walls they set large square towers and in the centre of the defended area they put great powerful buildings known as keeps. You can see these at places like Rochester in Kent or the Tower of London.

Castle design altered over the centuries and walls, towers and keeps were improved and strengthened. One of the biggest changes was in the shape of the towers which were made round, rather than square. When large cannon were introduced castles were no longer as important so that few were built after the 16th century, apart from towers (Martello towers) along the east coast, erected during the Napoleonic wars.

If you can walk, cycle or travel to a nearby castle you will be surprised at the number of interesting things to explore even amongst ruins. First of all look at the place where the castle stands – you will find that the position was carefully chosen for its strength. It is probably on a hill, by the side of a river, on a cliff or some other physical feature that would make it difficult for attackers. Stand there for a while and look at the gateway and see how strongly it is fortified. Notice the windows and see how small they are so that an archer could fire from them but it was difficult to aim into them. Notice the position of the towers and where the moat was. Is there a drawbridge and its tower at the crossing place?

Once inside the walls stand and look round the courtyard and imagine where the stables, armourer's shop, sheds and church probably stood. In this bailey was the strongest tower of all – the keep. Look for the doorway for this is often on the first floor so that attackers could not simply charge at the door but had to climb a staircase to get to it. Inside the hall you will probably find a large fireplace with a chimney rising up inside the wall. The floors were connected by spiral staircases for these took up less room and were difficult for an attacker to mount. Look at the walls themselves and notice how thick they are and how they are joined together. Remember that at the lower sections these walls are probably 10 – 12 feet thick.

If you can explore a castle you will certainly find them well worth all the effort. There are a number of books that will tell you about castles, and if you are visiting one you will probably find it more enjoyable if you read about that particular castle before you go, for then you know what to look for.

Churches

In most towns and villages the oldest building is likely to be the church and in them you can often see much of the local history so why not go exploring there? Remember that a church is a rather special place to many people and you should certainly treat it as such by being particularly quiet and respectful.

Stop outside first and look at the place. Has it a churchyard? If it has then walk round and look at the gravestones and read the epitaphs for they often tell you much about the church and the district around it. Look at the dates, for many will go back to the 18th century.

Now look up at the church itself. Has it a tower or a spire? What shape is the church and, more especially, what is the shape of the windows for these can tell you much about the date of the church. If the windows are small and round topped it probably means that at least part of the church dates back to the time of the Normans. Later a pointed arch and window were introduced and the style of their decoration will also tell you about the date of the church. If you look at books dealing with the style of buildings – architecture – they will give a rough guide to dates.

If you now enter the church stand just inside and look around for there is much to notice. Look again at the windows for they will probably be filled with stained glass and these are usually most beautiful. In the Middle Ages when so few people could read, these windows told them stories from the Bible and you will probably recognise many of the best known. Other favourite topics were the stories of saints. The colours were usually produced by mixing certain chemicals with ordinary glass when it was being made – this kind is known as pot metal – but there were other methods. The pieces of coloured glass were then secured by strips of lead which were roughly H-shaped in section and if you look closely at the windows you will see this method of construction.

Look down at the floor and you may be lucky enough to find there an example of those most interesting church features – brasses. These are sheets of brass cut into the shape of the figure, or else engraved with the picture of the person buried beneath it. There are many brasses scattered in churches all over Britain and many people are interested enough to take what are called rubbings.

To take a brass rubbing you need the same equipment as was used for the coal-hole covers – brush, paper, sticky tape and wax in the form called heelball. After cleaning the brass carefully it is covered with paper and then gently rubbed with the heelball and gradually the outline will become visible. Before you do any brass rubbing it is most important that you get the permission of the priest in charge of the church and this is best done by writing to him sometime beforehand.

Look at the door of the church as you stand in the porch for it may very well have some quite beautiful iron work in the form of hinges, bar, locks or decoration.

After looking at the church from the doorway stroll quietly around looking at walls, floors and ceilings for most churches will have some treasure in the way of chests, benches, lecterns, fonts and screens. A few churches have some rather special prizes, The explorer may find such things as pieces of armour and helmets hanging over the tomb of some local knight. On the wall you may well find plaques set there to commemorate a celebrity or local event of interest.

The Countryside

So far all the exploring has been concerned with towns but there are, of course, many things to see if you go exploring in the country or by the seaside.

In the country there are so many things to see that they would need a book on their own. We shall be considering bird watching later on and we have already mentioned plants and insects, but there are so many other things for the explorer to discover. Battlefields, windmills, market crosses, animals, abbeys, rivers, bridges, canals, watermills, motorways and a host of other things.

During the summer many people spend their holidays by the seaside and here too are grand places for exploring. Start on the beach and if you can find the space between all the holiday makers, take a stroll along by the sea's edge, preferably when the tide has gone out. Look out for shells, seaweeds and even pieces of driftwood for the water often rubs and moulds them into quite fascinating shapes. Look at the rock pools for these often contain a wide variety of treasures such as star fish, crabs, barnacles and seaweeds. They will have to be looked for since, more often than not, the creatures hide beneath rocks or burrow into the sand. A short piece of stick can be useful for turning over the rocks and probing into the sand. The seaweeds can be collected and preserved as suggested on page 26, but the creatures such as crabs are best left to themselves for it is extremely difficult to keep them alive in a tank.

If your seaside is anywhere near a port or the mouth of a river you may well be lucky enough to spot a number of ships passing. With a small pair of binoculars you can keep watch, recording the different types of ships, such as tankers, coastal steamers or perhaps even liners. Closer in shore you may be able to identify some sailing craft, motor boats and dinghies. If there are fishing boats about notice the letters on their sides for these identify the home port of the boats.

How about the town itself? Many towns such as Brighton were once only small fishing villages which grew into holiday resorts and a walk around that part of the town near the shore may well lead you to the older parts of the town, often with houses of weatherboard.

Is there a lifeboat station in the town? These are always

well worth visiting. Look out for coastguard stations and lighthouses which can be found in a few resorts.

There are many towns with long piers jutting out to sea for this was the only way in which passengers could get to the ships since the water was too shallow for them to come close into shore. Do not worry too much about the shops and amusement places on the pier, but look at the pier itself. Most were built many years ago so look for any dates and note the often rather fancy ironwork.

This has been a very quick survey of exploring in town and country but if you look through some of the following books there may well be many other ideas which you can follow up with interest and enjoyment.

Useful Books

Exploring the Seashore, Leslie Jackman. (Evans.)
'Discovering' Books (Shire Press).
Crosses; Civic Heraldry; Church Furniture; Wrought Iron; Brasses; Castles – Central England; Castles – Eastern England; Stained Glass; Watermills; Towns; This Old House; Windmills; Inn Signs.
'I Spy' Books (Dickens Press).
At the Seaside; On the Farm; In the Country; In the Street; On the Road; People and Places; On the Pavement.
Ladybird Books
The Seashore.
What to look for in Winter.
What to look for in Spring.
What to look for in Summer.
What to look for in Autumn.

Sports, Games and Pastimes

Athletics

One sport which requires an absolute minimum of equipment is athletics yet it is a very satisfying sport. There are several kinds of running races such as the short distance sprint where everything depends on speed in starting and perseverance in maintaining that speed in order to take the shortest possible time to cover a distance. Then there are the longer distances where stamina is probably more important than speed and finally there are the jumps (hurdles, long, high and pole vaulting). All forms of athletics demand training if you want good results and if you are unused to hard exercise it is important that you should break yourself in gradually by starting with fairly easy exercise periods and gradually increasing their length or difficulty. Distance running can be done on tracks or there is the tougher variety known as cross country running when the route lies across water, mud, woods, roads and farmyards. For this kind of running you need special shoes which are usually leather topped and fitted with spikes or small studs rather like football boots. Clothing needs to be light and comfortable and, as with walking, the socks are very important and must be well fitting or they can cause blistering. When not running it is important to keep warm and for this purpose a good track suit is desirable.

If you are really keen on running then you will probably get a great deal of pleasure and benefit from joining a club. Details of various local clubs can be obtained from the Amateur Athletics Association, 26, Park Crescent, London W.1.

Useful Books

Athletics, P. Hildreth. (Arco.)

Young Athlete's Companion, J. Disley. (Souvenir Press.)

Athletic Techniques – Running, J. H. Dodd. (Educational Productions.)

Athletic Techniques – Jumping, J. H. Dodd. (Educational Productions.)

Athletic Techniques – Throwing, J. H. Dodd. (Educational Productions.)

Ball Games

Playing with a ball is a very ancient way of amusing yourself and games such as tennis, football, cricket and netball are played by thousands of people every day. There are many other games in which a ball is used; these were, at one time, played by most children at school but now are largely forgotten. So why not try out some and perhaps ask your parents about the games they played as children.

Buttons

Five circles are drawn near a wall within the shape of a square with a fifth circle in the centre. In each circle is placed a button. The idea is to throw the ball so that it knocks a button out of a circle but the ball then has to bounce up, hit the wall, bounce back and be caught by the player. Each button knocked out of the circle belongs to the player but once the ball is dropped his opponent has a turn. Each player takes it in turn to provide the five buttons when his opponent is playing.

Cannon

A group of fivestones, or ordinary stones, are piled one on top of the other and the players are then divided into two teams; one defending and one attacking. The attackers stand a certain distance away and one then rolls the ball along the ground to knock down the pile of stones. If he is unsuccessful in, say, five tries the teams change over, but if the pile of stones is knocked over then all members of the attacking group scatter at once. The idea is now for the defenders to replace the stones in a pile whilst the attackers try to catch them by hitting them between shoulder and knee with the ball. Attackers may not run with the ball but can pass from one to another. As a defender is hit he is out of the game and if all the defenders are hit then the attackers have won, but if their opponents succeed in replacing the stones in a pile then they are the winners.

"Kingey"

All the players stand in a circle, legs slightly astride, with their feet touching and the ball is dropped in the centre and allowed to roll. The person between whose feet it rolls is now 'he'. The object is for 'he' to hit the others with the ball, again between shoulder and knee. Once a person is hit then they join with the original 'he' in catching the rest. The ball may be passed between those chasing but the runners may only knock the ball away with their clenched fist – not the open hand. As the game goes on there are more and more chasers after fewer and fewer runners and it takes an expert to stay uncaught for long.

Plain-Clap

This is an excellent game for developing a good eye and can be played anywhere that has a convenient wall. The player faces the wall and then throws the ball against it and catches it with both hands as it bounces back. Next it is thrown up and caught again but this time the hands are clapped before the ball is caught; next the player has to twist his hands round each other once before catching the ball, then the hands are folded across the chest before catching it and so on with hands touching shoulders, hips, heels and toe before catching the ball. Lastly the hands are cupped with fingers interlocked and the ball has to be caught with the palms turned outwards to the wall – the so-called 'egg in a basket'. The sequence can now be repeated but this time each move has to be preceded by one clap of the hands and the next sequence is preceded by a twist of the hands and so on. If the ball is dropped then somebody else has a turn and when that person is out then the first player starts at the beginning of the sequence in which the ball was dropped.

Dutch Rounders

Most people know how to play ordinary rounders but if you want a quick moving variety try Dutch rounders. In this game when any one person is out then the whole team is out but what makes it interesting is that play does not stop whilst the teams change over. If one of the players going out can grab the ball and hit the home post during the change over even before anybody has the chance to grab the bat, then the other team is out and everybody has to rush back again.

Skipping

French Skipping

This game calls for very quick footwork indeed and is especially enjoyable since you can introduce variations of your own. It is as well to wear slippers or shoes without buckles or anything that sticks out for these could make things far more difficult. You need a long loop of elastic, a piece about six feet long is quite good enough, but if you cannot get hold of a length of elastic you can join a number of rubber bands together. You now need two supporters – either friends or chairs will do – and these stretch out the elastic to make a loop raised about six inches from the floor. You now stand outside the loop facing towards one end and with a hop you lift the foot nearest the loop up and over and touch the ground inside the loop and then out again. You now lift the elastic with the outside of your foot and carry it across to the other side of the loop and touch the ground with your toe and, without stopping, back again. These two movements are repeated three times and you must not touch the second, straight strand of elastic with your foot. Then comes the jump when the elastic is carried over and the foot is placed on the ground so that the elastic encircles the ankle. Now you must jump up and clear your foot from the loop and land with both feet inside, or outside the main loop. This is the basic pattern which is now repeated with the other foot and if the entire routine is completed the loop is then raised higher above the ground and the routine repeated. Variations such as placing both feet within the loop for the final jump or using the hands instead of the feet to move the elastic are possible.

Dutch Skipping
This is a game for which you will certainly need some practice before you can succeed. You will need two skipping ropes and two friends whose job is to turn the ropes. The difficult part lies in turning two ropes at once so that they rotate in opposite directions without getting tangled. Both hands have to move at the same time but in the opposite directions and therein lies the skill. Once the ropes are going then you run in and continue skipping in the usual way except, of course, there are two ropes to worry about and this you will find no easy task.

Kite Flying

In many parts of the world flying kites is a very popular hobby with young and old and in Japan there is even a special kite festival. Competitions are held to find the highest flier or the most decorative kites, and there are even aerial fights with kites. There is a lot of fun to be had in getting a kite into the air, keeping it there and then coaxing it to go higher and higher. You can use ready-made ones or perhaps you might prefer to make your own. Bear in mind that the materials you use should be strong but light – strips of garden bamboo are useful for smaller kites and shelf or kraft paper is strong and cheap.

Starting with the simple, flat kite all that you need are two pieces of light wood, one longer than the other. These you fasten together in the form of a cross which now has to be covered with material. Lay the cross on your material and draw a line from tip to tip of the arms of the cross and this is the shape of the material you need. To secure it to the frame you can use glue along the arms or simply at the tips of the arms. For greater security you can tie thin cords from tip to tip of the frame and then fold the edge of the material over these and glue the fold-over tabs – if you use this method remember to leave an extra margin round the shape when you cut out the material. Next to be fitted is the harness string and this should be fastened to the longer arm of the framework and on to this harness will go the securing line. Lastly a tail of string tied with small 'bows' of paper is fitted to the bottom of the kite and this again is very important in balancing the kite so that you may find you need to adjust it after your first flights. Both harness and tail are needed to make the kite float in the air at just the right angle to get maximum lift.

Box kites can usually be relied on to give you a greater lift than flat kites but they are not as easy to make. You require four pieces of wood about 30 to 36 inches long and eight shorter pieces, say 10 to 12 inches long. These are joined together and the joints must be made reasonably strong for there will be some considerable pressure when the kite is in the air. When joining the pieces use one of the impact adhesives or a carefully positioned panel pin. It may help if you further strengthen the joint by binding it with Sellotape, gummed thread or twine. The basic shape is simply that of a hollow box and some extra rigidity can be obtained by fitting diagonal struts of cord from corner to corner. When you have finished making the framework you then cover it with an appropriate material but whatever you use must be stretched tight or else the kite will not rise properly.

The securing line for the kite needs to be fairly long and strong – some people like to use fishing line but thin twine or nylon cord will do very well. It should be secured to a winder so that there is less danger of the end slipping from your hand if the kite really rises well. A simple reel can be made from a flat piece of wood or you can push two pieces of dowel through a central bar.

Sometimes the kite will take off with no trouble at all but on other occasions it may be quite tricky to get it into the air. It helps if you have a friend to assist for he can hold the line while you run along with the kite held at arm's length above your head. It should be at a slight angle to the line of flight in order to get maximum lift. If you are on your own lay the winder down and run out a length of line and lay it on the ground for this relieves you of the difficulty of having to hold the winder and kite at the same time. You can now run along holding the kite and as soon as it begins to rise just let the line run through your hand. If the lift is really strong take care that the line does not run too quickly through your bare hands or you may well get a nasty burn. On windy days wear gloves or run the line under your foot so that you can tread on it to act as a brake.

One last word – if you are flying your kite in town do take great care to keep clear of any overhead telephone wires or power lines. Remember, it is illegal to fly your kite over 200 feet high.

Useful Books
Your Book of Kites, Clive Hart. (Faber.)

Model Aircraft

Most people have flown a paper aeroplane and know the thrill you get when it goes into a really good, long glide or a lucky twist and dive. Paper planes are fun but rather restricted in their performance so why not be a bit more ambitious. You can get very simple models made of a light porous wood called balsa, or you can cut one yourself from a thin board of the balsa. Draw the outline and cut it out with one of the modelling knives available in most model or 'do-it-yourself' shops. The wing is inserted in a slot cut through the body. If you cut a notch near the nose you can launch the plane by means of an elastic band. You will find that some experimenting is needed before you can get the balance just right.

More ambitious gliders can be made up from kits which

use a balsa wood framework covered with thin, tough material rather like thin plastic sheeting. Some such models can be quite large and given a good up-draught will cover long distances. The drawback with all gliders is that they depend on rising air and cannot be controlled once they are launched, if you want to control them then the aircraft must have an engine. Modern designs are so good that small engines can now deliver quite a powerful thrust. Although it is possible to construct a complete engine it is far simpler to buy one ready made and fit it into one of the kits available from model shops. The prices vary considerably and naturally depend on how complicated the models are.

There are three types of powered model aircraft and the choice is entirely yours, each has its advantages and its drawbacks. First there are those that fly free and this means that the control surfaces are set, the engine started and the plane is launched; it will now follow a set course until the fuel supply runs out and the engine stops. For distance work this is a very good method but if you want the plane to perform aerobatics and carry out any sort of manoeuvres then you must have controlled flight.

Line flight means that the plane is captive and secured to your hand by a grip to which wires are attached and these alter controls in the plane. This system means that your model will fly in circles around you and can also be controlled to perform some manoeuvres.

The most exciting of all methods and, of course, the most expensive, is to use radio control. In this system a small radio transmitter is held by the controller and the signals it sends out are picked up by a small receiver in the plane and used to alter the controls. The transmitter is usually fitted with a series of buttons which you press to turn the aircraft whilst others have controls which can be adjusted to make the aircraft perform more complicated aerobatics.

Whatever type of plane you decide to use there are one or two precautions to take when flying it. Obviously you need a large, clear space for it is so easy for the plane to become entangled or lost and this danger is greatest with the free flight aircraft. With a line controlled aircraft there is hardly any danger of losing it but it is easy to hit something accidentally. Unless they are anchored to a fixed point it means that you have to turn round all the time and this can make you a little dizzy if you go on for too long.

Useful Books
Your Book on Aero Modelling, **R. R. Rodwell.** (Faber.)
Modern Aeromodelling, R. Moulton. (Faber.)
Radio controlled models, R. H. Warring. (Museum Press.)

Model Boats

To fly a model aircraft you only need space but for model boats you obviously need a fairly large area of water and this can be a big drawback. Rivers and streams are not necessarily good places as the currents may well carry your craft away. The ideal places are ponds either artificial or natural, although here you need to take care that there are not too many weeds or your boat may get its propeller or keel entangled. Check the water for currents by throwing a small twig on to the surface and watch whether it moves quickly. For weeds and so on a stick dipped in the water near the edge may well tell you.

Like aircraft there are three types of model boats, free sailing, powered and controlled. Free sailing boats are almost invariably powered by the wind and sails and this does mean that there is a danger that the boat may well be left becalmed in the centre of the pond. It is as well to have a long stick or a good pair of wellington boots otherwise you may have a long wait ahead of you. Some people suggest tying a nylon line to the boat but this does slow it down and it may get entangled with other boats.

Powered model boats can be made in the form of tugs, liners or motor boats and most are driven by small but quite powerful electric motors worked off batteries. These are less likely to get stuck in the centre of the pond unless they break down or the batteries go flat so you should always check the motor and batteries before you launch the vessel. For the real expert enthusiast there are a few models that work from real steam engines but they are complicated and expensive.

The third class of vessels are the radio controlled ones and again these are expensive but certainly they are the most exciting for you can steer them and alter speed. In model aircraft it is important that the equipment should be as small and light as possible but with boats it can all be much bigger and more complicated so it is possible to provide a greater variety of movements.

Yachts are the most common of all types of sailing boats and these can range from simple, small craft, to boats several feet long with complex sails. Like the large real yachts they can be fitted with automatic steering devices so they keep to a set course. These devices work by altering the rudder setting by means of small sail attached to the stern.

You may well try making your own model boat for there is much satisfaction in watching a boat of your creation sailing across the broad pond. You can buy kits to make up your model or you can, if you are skilled, build the entire boat.

Useful Books
Model Boats for Beginners, M. Gilmore. (Harper.)
Power Model Boats, V. Smeed. (Aeronautical Press.)

Riding

One of the most popular pastimes, especially amongst girls, is horse riding and its associated activities of jumping and pony trekking. Most of the organised pony treks can be done by people who have never sat a horse before although there is no doubt that someone with experience will enjoy the trek more than a beginner.

If you feel that you might like to try one of the many organised treks you can write to one or more of these addresses and they will supply you with details.

The Central Council of Physical Recreation
6, Bedford Square, London W.C.1.

The Ponies of Britain Club
Brookside Farm, Ascot, Berkshire.

The Youth Hostels Association
Trevelyan House, St. Albans, Herts.

Each trek differs in its arrangements but most will expect you to look after your pony's harness (riders call this tack), watering and feeding but as each trek has a qualified leader all this will be fully explained to you and you will find it fun. Most of the trips are made in reasonable stages but if you are

CURRY-COMB

fresh to riding you may find it a little bone shaking and wearing at first, but soon you will be enjoying the excitement of a holiday that is different.

Pony trekking is probably only a 'once a year' event but you may feel that you would like to take up riding as a full-time hobby. For most of us it is not possible to have our own pony and this means using a riding school. The number of lessons that you can manage will obviously depend on the cost and this does vary from school to school but it usually pays to pick the best that you can afford. It is also rather nice to have a complete riding outfit but again this is not absolutely necessary although a protective hat is essential and this should be your first purchase. It is a fairly simple matter to learn how to ride but it is very much a matter of practice making perfect and the more you ride the better you become.

When you have gained some proficiency in the skill of riding you may care to try some simple gymkhana activities and these are great fun, with races and competitions.

Finally, jumping is another activity that you can try but again it is something that needs practice and careful teaching.

Useful Books
Pony Trekking for All, J. Kerr Hunter. (Nelson.)
Ponycraft, A. Bullen. (Blandford.)
Progressive Steps in Riding, P. Churchill. (Blandford.)
Riding for Everybody, P. Churchill. (Blandford.)
Your Book of Keeping Ponies, J. Holyoake. (Faber.)
'*I Spy*' Books (Dickens Press).
Horses and Ponies.

Growing Things

One of the most important events in man's history was his discovery of crop growing. Although it happened many thousands of years ago man has been growing things ever since. With so many people living in flats it is not easy for them to enjoy the pleasures of gardening but even if there is no room for a full-sized garden you might still be able to manage a window box!

Gardening is not something that you can just start without preparation; if you feel that you would like to take it up as a pastime then it is important to do some reading and planning before you start or you may be disappointed with your results. Plants are pretty hardy but they do need help and attention for their growth may be affected by many things. Some plants do better in one soil than another so that you will certainly need to know the type of soil that you have in your area. If it is an acid soil then plants such as azaleas will do badly; if the soil has a lot of clay in it then it will be good for roses. To find out the nature of the soil in your garden ask at the local park or library and they will advise you.

If you are taking over an unused plot of ground for your garden the very first step must be to clear it of bricks and other rubbish. If there are any odd branches, twigs and leaves make a bonfire and keep the ashes for they can be used to help make the plants grow stronger. When the patch is thoroughly cleared turn over the earth and mix in the ashes. You can now begin to consider what you want to grow and where you want to place the different plants.

Apart from flowers you may like to grow something a little different such as herbs, vegetables or perhaps you might like to build up a rockery or create a small pond in your garden.

A pond can be very simple with little more than a basin and a stone or two but, if you can afford it, you can have one with a waterfall, fountain, or other extras which can be bought in a gardening shop. For the simplest kind, all you need is a hole and something to line it with to make it water-tight; a small but perfectly satisfactory pond can be made by setting a large, plastic bowl into the ground. For something larger you will need to dig a bigger hole and line it with some material, probably the cheapest and simplest of all is thick plastic sheeting.

Dig out an appropriately sized hole and make sure that the sides and bottom are clear of any sharp stones or anything that might tear the plastic. Lay the sheeting over the hole (if you have enough plastic use a double layer) and gently smooth the plastic down to cover the bottom and sides. Some of the plastic will overlap at the surface but this part can be pegged to the ground and covered with earth or stones to hide it from view. Before you begin any elaborate preparations to stock the pond with plants and fish it is as well to fill it with water and then leave it for some time to make sure that there are no serious leaks.

When you are sure that the basin of the pond is satisfactory then you can begin to stock it with plants and soil. If you simply pile earth in you will find that the water gets very muddy so it is better to use some clean, washed stones and sand mixed with loam, bone meal and leafmould. Water plants can be pushed into the layer of soil at the bottom of the pond; at first you may need to tie them to stones until they are well rooted. Fish have to get used to the pond so don't put too many in too soon and don't forget that some cats are good fishers so you may need to fit some wire netting around the edges of your pond. If you want a more elaborate pond then you can, of course, build the sides up with cement although this can be quite a tricky job. Another, easier, way is to buy one of the fibre-glass water containers which are ideal, being strong, hard wearing and very nicely shaped. However they are expensive.

To go round the edge of your pond you might like a simple rockery but it should be in a sunny spot since most rock plants do not grow well in the shade. Find some good sized stones and push them into the earth leaving the ends projecting with a gap between them so that the roots of the plants can find room to grow and spread. You will get the best results if you set the stones more or less horizontally. There are many plants that are suitable for a rockery and flowering in a variety of colours. Creeping Jenny is gold whilst saxifrage can be had in almost any shade from red to white, Alpine phlox produces very attractive blue flowers and there are many other kinds.

For the main part of the garden there are flowers that are so sturdy that they will grow almost in spite of the efforts of most gardeners. For quite a small sum of money you can buy a supply of seeds of the so-called hardy annuals and these plants will do well in most soils. Before you plant these seeds make sure that there are no lumps of earth in the plot. You will help them grow if you sprinkle the soil with a fertilizer; these are mixtures containing chemicals which the plants need to make them grow big and strong. There are many different kinds and you should ask the shopkeeper which one he thinks best for your type of flowers.

Now make a groove in the soil, not too deep, using a pointed stick or the edge of a trowel and drop the seeds in; make very sure that you don't get too many seeds too close together or the young plants will choke one another. When the seeds are all in place in the groove use a rake, a stiff brush or your hands and cover them with earth and then press it down gently – not too tight. They will now want watering but don't soak them, just give them a good sprinkling from a watering can or, if you haven't one of these, use a tin or plastic bottle with holes punched in the bottom with a nail.

If you are lucky the plants will soon begin to push through and if you bought a mixed packet of seeds you may find that you have cornflowers, nasturtiums, larkspur or other types. The seed packet or a gardening book will probably have pictures which will help you discover the names of the various plants.

Annuals are plants which bloom only once whereas perennials are supposed to blossom year after year as indeed they should for they are tough and long lasting. Most perennials should last at least four or five years and need little or no attention. This group of plants include marigolds, lupins and delphiniums, varieties which you probably know already.

The typical English flower is, of course, the rose and most gardeners like to include some of these among their plants and although roses prefer a clay soil they will flourish in others. If you want to go in for roses it is probably best to buy your bushes from a good nurseryman – a man who sells plants. When you get them home look over the roots and clip off any broken or damaged pieces. If the plants look very dry then give them a soak in a bucket of water for an hour or so. Now dig a hole in your garden about 12 inches across and, after opening out the roots of the bush, place it in the hole and replace the earth. The rose bush will certainly do a little better if you mix some damp peat or bone meal with the soil as you replace it in the hole; now tread down the earth firmly round the plant but do not stamp it down.

One of the secrets of successful rose growing is the careful cutting of the twigs – gardeners call this pruning. This is a job which has to be done with skill and courage but, above all, with knowledge and it is important that you find out as much as possible about it before you start or you could well ruin the plant. Read about it in one of the books listed on page 68 and if you are unsure ask for advice.

If you have room in your garden you might like to try growing a few shrubs, which are bushes that produce large numbers of flowers. They are pretty tough and once they take root and begin growing they will last for many years with little or no attention. They like plenty of light and air so space them out well. They do need an occasional pruning as the flowers die off, but again it is best to read some of the gardening books before you tackle this job. Shrubs have one great advantage in that many of them will flower long after other plants have finished their displays. Winter jasmine is usually still at its best during November when almost every other plant appears dead. Some of the most popular varieties of shrubs are honeysuckle, buddleias, jasmine, Virginia creeper, rhododendrons and lilacs.

Although flowers are beautiful and attractive you may like to grow some plants which are of practical use such as herbs and vegetables; certainly the cook of the family will be pleased if you decide to do so. However, if you have a heavy clay soil in your district you will find that herbs, apart from mint, won't do very well. The patch of ground you choose for your herbs should be well protected from the wind for they like to be warm.

To start off your herb garden turn over the soil and dig in some compost which you make by piling up all your grass cuttings, old leaves, flowers, clippings and so on and leaving them to rot for several months. If you cannot wait this long then use a fertilizer which you can buy from a shop. Most herbs grow from seeds which have to be planted each year so buy a packet or two ready for sowing in March. Plant them in boxes of earth which should be kept in a greenhouse, or some other warm spot. The young plants can be planted out in the garden in May when the weather should be better.

There are dozens of herbs that you can grow. You may decide to concentrate on just one type or you can grow one or two samples from each group. To get the flavour of herbs in cooking only a leaf or two is required for each meal so that you can grow many types including sage, mint, rosemary, parsley and chives. Other herbs are noted for their smells such as thyme, rue, rosemary, lavender and heliotrope. Most herbs are grown for their leaves whilst from others only the flower is used in seasoning so that the best way of collecting and using the herbs does vary and you will need to refer to the books to find out which part of the plant you have to collect. Herbs can be used fresh from the garden during the summer or they can be dried for winter use. This is best done slowly in a warm cupboard or room.

Vegetable growing is a job that requires a lot of hard work and plenty of space so don't start a vegetable garden unless you are determined to persevere with it. Peas, runner beans, spinach, shallots, leeks, lettuces and rhubarb can all be cultivated but it is as well to give a good deal of thought to your choice before you start. Don't forget too that you will be engaged in a more or less continuous struggle with the birds as to who eats the fine crop that you raise!

Bulbs are a special class of plants and these can be grown either indoors or out-of-doors. Some bulbs once planted can be left and they will bloom year after year – this group includes snowdrops, daffodils, crocus among others. Other bulbs, once they have bloomed and the leaves have died, have to be dug up and stored until the following year when they can be replanted – dahlias and tulips are in this group. The time of year to plant the bulbs is important and must be decided well in advance for you must know when they are due to bloom. Those flowering in the autumn must be put in the ground during the summer, those blooming in the summer must be planted in the spring and the spring flowers need to be put in during the preceding autumn.

Window boxes

Perhaps you have read all these suggestions about the garden and are thinking that they are of no use to you since you live in a flat and have no garden at all. Even so, you can still go in for gardening. If you have a balcony of any sort you can place tubs or troughs on it and fill them with earth to hold your plants. If you have no balcony then you could, perhaps,

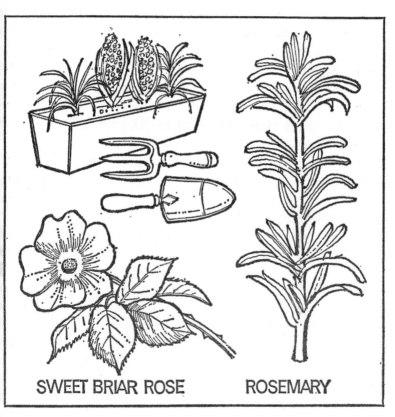

SWEET BRIAR ROSE   ROSEMARY

make do with window boxes. If, however, you decide on window boxes you must make sure that they are *absolutely safe and well secured* for a falling flowerpot can be a deadly menace. If you have tubs or window boxes then you will need to choose your plants carefully for not all types will grow well in these cramped conditions. You could try some bulbs or fuchsias and geraniums.

If you decide to go gardening you will certainly find it a very busy and rewarding pastime and one that will bring pleasure to yourself and others.

Useful Books
Enjoy making a Garden out of Nothing, C. A. Lejune. (Gollancz.)
Gardens and Gardening, Janet Drysdale. (Studio Vista.)
Your Book of Gardening, C. Cowell. (Faber.)
Your First Garden, G. R. Kingbourne. (Dobson.)
Gardening for Fun, G. Scurfield. (Faber.)
'I Spy' Books (Dickens Press).
Garden Flowers.
'Discovering' Books (Shire Press).
Herbs; The Folklore of Plants.

Bird Watching

Have you ever looked at a bird? Not your budgerigars or canaries but a free, wild bird? No matter where you live in town or country you are certain to have birds about you for they are one of the most numerous of creatures. Some species have wings which stretch out to a width of more than ten feet whilst others are no more than a few inches across. There are birds of every colour and with beaks of all shapes and sizes, there are even some birds that cannot fly! In this country we do not have the most unusual types but even so there are dozens of different species many of which can be seen even in the middle of a big town.

The ways in which birds behave are most interesting and thousands of people all over the country spend their spare time watching and recording their details. On a fine day sit yourself by the window and just keep an eye on the birds, they will probably be sparrows and pigeons. You will be surprised by some of the strange and interesting movements of individual birds and if you have a garden then you will almost certainly spot several types you probably never noticed before. Here, then, is a hobby that costs practically nothing to start or continue and you can do it almost anywhere out of doors. All you need to begin with are your eyes and plenty of patience. Later you will probably want to acquire some form of magnifying device like a telescope or a pair of binoculars. They need not be very powerful or expensive but they do enable you to see so much more. By the way, if you can, choose a light-weight pair for you are going to hold them to your eyes for some time and there is no sense in straining your arms. Telescopes usually have a much smaller field of view than glasses and are, therefore, a little difficult to keep on a moving target. As with several other hobbies you will need to record your findings, use your clip board for this and when you get home copy out your quick notes tidily and carefully into a book or on to cards. When you are actually watching a bird it is best to keep your eyes on it and only make your notes when it flies away – if you take your eyes off it to write you may well miss something interesting. It is best to make a very full record giving the type of bird, where and when you saw it, what it was doing, unusual features and anything else worth noting.

In town the most common species are sparrow, pigeon, starling and blackbird but if you can get out into the country or park then there will be birds that you can't recognise at once. How do you identify these? The most useful tool is a good book. There are lots in the shops but the best thing to do is to go along to the library and look at all they have, pick the one that you feel is the most useful and then save up to buy a copy of your own.

The books usually have their own ideas on how to make the task of identification easier but whichever scheme is used it will depend on certain points. Size, shape, beaks, legs, colour and song are all useful clues in discovering the identity of the mystery flyer.

Beaks can tell you a great deal about the bird; insect catching birds usually have fairly pointed beaks but seed-eaters have shorter, tougher pointed beaks. Fish-catching birds have long, rather thin pointed beaks and there are many varieties of shape, length and width. If you can get along to a zoo or big aviary make a point of looking at some of the really curious birds like spoonbills and pelicans!

Legs and feet can also tell the watcher more about the bird. Webbed feet belong to a water bird whereas perching birds have their claws arranged with three pointing forward and one backwards – like your budgerigar – to grip the branch. Woodpeckers have their claws arranged in pairs, two forward and two back, so that they can grip a flat surface whilst hanging on to the side of the tree. Long legs belong to birds who spend part of their life standing in water – the waders. Necks and body shape are also useful identification points as is the colouring and feather arrangement.

Most birds have a song or call and you may like to try recording their songs and with present-day battery driven tape recorders it is much easier to do this. To obtain the best results you really need a top quality microphone but quite good results can be obtained from ordinary instruments if you use them correctly and carefully. It is important to reduce the background noises as much as possible and for this you need some form of sound focusing device. A simple, cheap and reasonably efficient horn can be made from kitchen foil which is formed into a cone shape. The microphone is placed at the narrow end so cutting out most of the noise from the back and sides. Better results will be obtained if you can arrange the microphone so that it points into the horn for this focuses the sound even more finely. There are a number of very fine records of bird songs which can help you identify any unknown sounds.

It may be that you are lucky enough to find a nest with eggs in it and this will give you a wonderful chance to follow a bird's early life at first hand. On no account disturb the nest and certainly don't take any of the eggs. Since you don't want to upset or drive away the parents it is important that they should get used to you and it will help if you can erect a 'hide'. This is simply some cover behind which you can stay out of sight. It need only be an old piece of plastic sheeting, blanket or some leafy branches stuck into the ground. Place your hide in position and leave it for a while and in this way the birds get used to it and you can quietly take up your position and watch them at any time.

The birds that you can watch will depend very much on the part of the country in which you live and the time of year, for many birds fly away and others arrive at set times of the year. Sometimes our visitors arrive in flocks and others come individually, but it is an incredible fact that although the bird may fly thousands of miles it can still find its way back to its old nesting ground.

At different times of the year the birds carry out different jobs such as nest building, hatching and rearing their young and it may well be that you can follow the life of one particular family for a full year.

There are a number of bird sanctuaries dotted about the country and it is possible to visit these and this gives you a wonderful chance to see some of the less common types of birds. If you want to find out about these write to the group listed on the next page.

You can also combine one or two other activities such as photography and sketching with your hobby of bird watching. You will find these two activities described on pages 85 and 89.

COAL TIT

CIRL BUNTING

Useful Books
Collins Pocket Guide to British Birds, R. S. Fitter. (Collins.)
Collins Pocket Guide to Bird Watching, R. S. Fitter. (Collins.)
Pictorial Encyclopedia of Birds, J. Hanzak. (Hamlyns.)
Birds of the London Area, London Natural History Society. (Rupert Hart Davies.)
Bird Watching, Hockely Clarke. (Pelham Books.)
Watching Birds, James Fisher. (Collins.)
'I Spy' Books (Dickens Press).
Birds.

Useful Address
The Young Ornithologists' Club.
   The Lodge, Sandy, Beds.

You will find a complete list of all the bird sanctuaries in the British Isles in *Where to Watch Birds* by John Gooders. (André Deutsch.)

Doing Things

Astronomy

To the Ancients the heavens were filled with gods and goddesses. They had many stories to explain the stars and they saw them as making shapes connected with these stories. We still use their names for these groups of stars – constellations – and on a clear night it is fairly easy to pick out many of the brighter groups. The study of the heavens is known as astronomy and it is one that amateurs can excel in; several discoveries have been made by amateurs. One of the best known astronomers is Patrick Moore who is an amateur.

To most people astronomy suggests great telescopes peering up into the sky but you can see a great deal without a telescope or even binoculars. Charts of the night sky are available which show all the stars that you can see with the naked eye so they are ideal for the amateur. These star maps show the constellations and indicate where you can find them in the sky. Other maps, often published by newspapers such as *The Times* and *The Daily Telegraph*, show the changes in the sky month by month as planets alter their positions; stars also move but so slowly that they seem to stand still.

If you live near the centre of a big town you will, unfortunately, not be able to see as much as somebody who lives in the country as the street lamps and house lights tend to blot out many of the less brilliant stars. However, if you choose good, cloudless evenings on which to watch you will still see much to interest you.

Since scientists have been able to send rockets to the moon we have learnt much about this satellite and complete maps

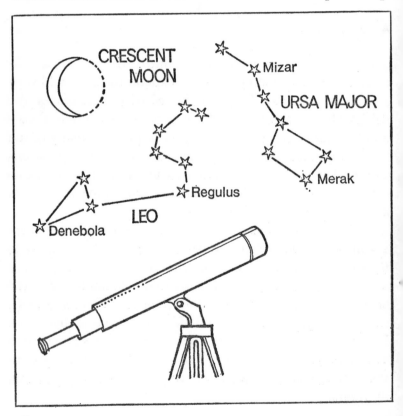

have been made of its surface. On many nights you will be able to locate the area of some of the so-called seas and identify them by name. If you want to see the moon craters in detail then you will need some magnifying device such as opera glasses, binoculars or a telescope. Even the smallest opera glasses will enable you to see much more than with the naked eyes including many more stars as well as some of the more distant planets. Binoculars which are usually at least four times as powerful as opera glasses, will let you see craters on the moon and the shape of the rings around Saturn.

Remember that you must never ever try to look at the sun with a telescope or magnifier.

Modern methods have made it possible to produce quite powerful telescopes very cheaply and you might like to save up and buy one. With telescopes and binoculars it is important to make sure they are held very firmly or you will find it difficult to keep your target in view. If you do not have a stand on which to fix them then steady them against a tree, wall or window frame.

At first you will probably be quite happy just to look around the heavens but after a while you will probably want to do something a little more useful. If you become really interested you may like to join the British Astronomical Association and if you write to the Assistant Secretary at 303, Bath Road, Hounslow West, Middlesex, you can ask for details of the Association.

Useful Books
The Times Guide to the Sky at Night, N. Wymer. (Hamish Hamilton.)

The Sky at Night, Patrick Moore. (Eyre & Spottiswoode.)
Vol. 1, Vol. 2.
Astronomy with Binoculars, J. Muirden. (Faber & Faber.)
'I Spy' Books (Dickens Press).
Sky.

Angling

Most people imagine fishing – it should really be called angling – as a nice, quiet hobby, just sitting on a river bank watching a float bobbing up and down on the water. This is just one aspect of the hobby but there are many other approaches to this sport and you can make it restful and simple or energetic and complicated to suit yourself. You can enjoy game fishing, that is going after trout, and salmon, or the easier, coarse fishing which covers all other types of fresh water fish. If you like you can also try sea fishing.

You can begin with a stick, a piece of string and a worm and you may well catch something, but if you want to do some real fishing then you will need some better equipment. It is possible to spend a great deal of money on your tackle (this is what anglers call their equipment), but it is possible to manage quite well with some quite cheap items. Before you buy anything have a talk with an angling friend or read some of the books listed. What you need to buy will depend on the type of fishing you intend to do so this is also something to decide beforehand, but whatever your choice, you will need a rod, a line and some hooks. There are three main types of rod; split cane, fibre glass and steel. For most types of fishing rods of cane or fibre glass are probably most useful. Fibre glass rods need little care and attention for the material is tough and unaffected by water. The size of your rod will be determined by the kind of fish you are after.

On to the rod goes a reel to hold the line and again you can get a simple drum type or those fitted with gadgets to control the run of line, the speed at which you can rewind and other refinements. The line itself is now almost always nylon which is light and tough.

Most important are the hooks for without these you will never catch anything! They come in various sizes and shapes and are graded by numbers; those with a low number are the larger sizes.

In addition to these main items you can add any number of extras including creels to hold your catch; floats with wonderful names like coffin, Arlesey bomb and drilled bullet; and nets.

Now that you have your equipment you probably want to rush off and start fishing but there is one more thing you must have before you can make a start. It is the law in Britain that you need a fishing licence before you can cast your hook into most waters. It doesn't cost much as a rule unless you are after salmon. There is one other very important fact and that is, even with a licence you still need permission from the landowner if the river in which you fish runs through his land. There may be a charge for this privilege, as well.

At certain times of the year you are not allowed to catch some species of fish. You can find out these details from one of the many books on angling.

Many young anglers fish in ponds and lakes and the fish found in there such as perch, tench, rudd and pike can provide a great deal of sport. Some of these fish grow to a fair size and if you are lucky enough to hook a big one your line and rod need to be strong. In many rivers you will find a great variety of fish – barbel, bream, chub, dace and roach. Some will be found in fast flowing rivers whilst others prefer slow running streams.

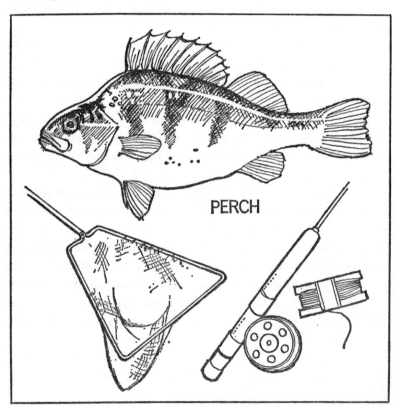

PERCH

Trout are a favourite fish for keen anglers but they need a special technique for trout like to eat flies. To catch a trout you have to try and copy the movements and appearance of a fly with your hook. The hook has to pass over the surface and move like an insect so that the trout will rise and take the bait, this technique of throwing the 'fly' hook is known as casting. There are a variety of designs for the flies and most anglers have their own favourites and many make their own.

Bait is most important for it is this that makes the fish bite and so take the hook and again most anglers have one or two types that they claim will produce the best results. Bread paste, worms and maggots are probably the commonest but cheese, wheat and other unusual things are also used.

A word about your clothing when you go fishing. Make sure that you have warm clothing with you for it can get very chilly when you are standing about. An anorak or similar garment is very useful for they are particularly good at keeping out the wind. For your feet you should have a pair of rubber boots but, if you can afford them, it is probably as well to get some thigh waders for this means that you will not be bothered with any danger of wet feet!

If you are new to the sport of angling you will probably enjoy it even more if you join one of the many angling clubs for the members are usually very ready to help newcomers.

One last word – water can be dangerous so if you plan to fish make sure that you can swim – if you fall in then the worst you will get is a wetting.

Useful Books
Angling, Clive Gamman. (Arco.)

Teach Yourself Fishing, T. Rodway. (E.U.P.)
Freshwater Fishing, B. Venables. (Herbert Jenkins.)
The Anglers' Handbook, R. Arnold. (Arthur Barker.)
The Art of Angling, Trevor Housby. (Evans.)
The Anglers' Pocket Book, J. Wentworth Day. (Evans.)

Archaeology

Parts of the story of man's past was, for a long time, covered in mystery. No one knew why small hills stood in the middle of fields or groups of stones stood about. These, and other mysteries, have now been solved by some rather special detectives. These experts examine clues and build up their knowledge slowly and with great care, making sure that nothing is disturbed before they have recorded its position and other details; these 'history detectives' are called archaeologists.

There are many local societies, large and small, all over the country which encourage their members to become amateur archaeologists and you might well like to take part in this activity. Many societies arrange visits to places of special interest and arrange for talks to be given by experts. There are few parts of Britain where you cannot see something of interest ranging from the great stones of Stonehenge to burial hills, or flint mines like Grimes Graves in Norfolk. Not all archaeologists are concerned with prehistoric things and today there is a growing interest in the remains of old factories and mines which were working during the last century – this new study is usually called industrial archaeology. A great deal of work is now going on in this field and you might like to do some of the measuring and recording which is so necessary.

Whichever field of archaeology you are interested in you must have a great deal of patience for careless or hasty work could ruin something that can never be replaced.

You may be lucky enough to take part in an excavation – archaeologists call them digs – and these are always interest-

ing. Naturally there are one or two trained archaeologists in charge to plan and direct the whole operation. The project is very carefully organised and digging is only carried out working to a plan, each digger concentrating on a small section. It is most important that the digging is done slowly and carefully for a careless jab with a spade could shatter a pot which has lain undisturbed for 3,000 years. Much of the earth has to be removed by using a brush or by blowing it away. If you are fortunate enough to come across something in the ground during a dig do not remove it but report your discovery to the person in charge. Before the find is removed its exact position, depth, angle and appearance must be recorded. Most digs provide all the equipment that you need but don't forget to go along in your old clothes for you will certainly get very dirty. A small gardening trowel and a hand brush will always be useful for removing loose soil from any discoveries.

If you would like to take up this most interesting and useful occupation look through the books listed below for the address of your local society or ask at your library.

Useful Books
Collins Field Guide to Archaeology in Britain, E. S. Wood. (Collins.)
Instruction in Archaeology, A. V. Gibson. (Museum Press.)
Approach to Archaeology, S. Piggott. (A. & C. Black.)
'*I Spy*' *Books* (Dickens Press).
Archaeology.

Photography

One picture is worth ten thousand words. Few people would not agree with this old Chinese saying and a photograph can often tell you more than several pages of writing. Photography is a very important and useful hobby for apart from the pleasure and fun it offers it enables you to record a thing, a scene or an event that might otherwise be lost forever. You can also use it when carrying out some of the other pastimes discussed in this book.

Modern cameras are simple and so efficient that you should be able to get good pictures every time. If you know something about your camera and what it can do then you will almost certainly be able to improve your pictures.

The photograph we look at is produced by a film in a camera so let us look at the films first. There are two common sizes, 120 which is used in the majority of 'box' cameras and 35mm which is smaller and is used by many of the more expensive cameras. Films also vary in their speed and this means that a 'fast' film is capable of taking pictures even when the subject is not very brightly lit. At one time most films took only black and white pictures but over the last few years colour films have become much more common. They are more expensive than black and white but for some types of pictures, such as views, they are invaluable. Some colour films give colour pictures whilst another type produces slides or transparencies which have to be looked at through a special viewer or else projected on a screen. Before you take any photographs you should decide which kind of film will give you the best results for that particular job. Another important thing to remember is that films are affected by light so keep all of them, new or used, out of direct, bright light or you will find that all your pictures will be 'fogged', that is slightly discoloured. By the way, always treat your developed film – the negatives – with care for any scratches or marks can spoil the picture when you have them printed.

Most people take their films to the chemist to have them developed and printed but it is fairly easy to do these jobs yourself if you learn the process. Some of the books listed below will tell you more about this subject.

Obviously to take photographs you must have a camera and there are hundreds of different types to choose from. You can buy them at anything from a few shillings to a few hundred pounds. Generally speaking, the more your camera costs the more it is able to do.

Simplest of all are the 'box' type cameras, most using a 120 film. This type has what is called a fixed focus which means that you do not have to alter the lens no matter how far away your subject is. It also means that you cannot take close up pictures. The shutter which you operate to take your picture is also set and this means that you can only take pictures if the light is fairly good.

Next come those slightly more expensive cameras which have about three settings for the lens depending on the distance away from the subject. Such cameras often have a little slide or similar device which you have to set according to how bright the light is.

The next group of cameras are more complicated and may have a lens which has to be focused for each shot; the shutter also has several settings and you will need to read the instruction book carefully to find out about the correct use of lens and shutter.

Polaroid cameras are a special group which differ from ordinary cameras for they produce a finished picture without having to take out the film and have it developed and printed by the chemist. After each picture is taken you can see the finished result in a matter of minutes by following the simple instructions. There is one snag for the polaroid films are more expensive than ordinary films.

A great help to the photographer is 'flash' which means producing a very bright light which lasts for only a very short time. To do this we need a special bulb which is used only once and then is thrown away and this needs a special gadget known as a flash gun which is often fitted on to the camera. Flash is very useful but it does need a little care in its use or the pictures will have a 'soot and whitewash' look with everything either very black or very white. You will need to practise and experiment in order to get the best results.

Whatever type of camera you have there are one or two simple ways of improving your photographs. Many pictures are spoilt because they are fuzzy and blurred. This may be because the lens is poor which is often the case with very cheap cameras but the most usual reason is camera shake. This means that as the picture was being taken the camera moved very slightly. To avoid this when taking your picture rest the camera on something solid, like a tree, wall or chair. If this is not possible then grip the camera firmly and, as you press the shutter, hold your breath. If you are going to do a lot of photography it might be as well to purchase a tripod. It also helps if you plan your picture and, as you look through the view-finder of your camera, try to position yourself so that the picture looks interesting. Make sure that your view-finder is filled without too many empty and uninteresting spaces. Decide what the main item of your picture is and make sure that this is near the centre so that it stands out. Keep an eye open for unusual effects such as a branch, a bunch of leaves, a wall, an open door, or something similar which can serve as part of a frame for your photograph.

As you move your camera about looking for good 'shots' take care that you do not point the camera directly into the sun or your pictures will not be very good.

You will probably find it useful, especially when you start using a new camera, if you list the details of the photographs you take. These should include time of day, weather, whether it was bright or dull and other similar information. If you do this you can then look at the negatives and see which ones are the best. This comparison will enable you to decide which timing and planning gives the best results for your camera.

One big drawback to photography is that it can be an expensive hobby so practise using the empty camera until you can operate all controls with ease.

If you remember the simple rules listed above and read some of the books listed below you will begin to get a much more detailed understanding of your hobby and as well as producing better pictures you will also save yourself money.

Useful Books
Instructions to Young Photographers, H. Rogers. (Museum Press.)

Picture Making with Your Camera, M. Lillington Hall. (Newnes.)

Teach Yourself Photography, S. W. Bowler. (E.U.P.)

Using Your Camera, R. Clark. (Oldbourne.)

Polaroid Guide, W. D. Emanuel & L. A. Mannheim. (The Focal Press.)

Sketching

You may not fancy the technical problems involved in taking photographs but you might still like to be able to record scenes and details. If this is the case why not try sketching? You may find that you have a skill in this form of art and if so you will find that sketching is very satisfying. Before you decide that you can't draw have a go – you may well be surprised with what you can do.

Before you start out on your first sketching trip it will be as well to do a little practice and preparation at home. First of all you obviously need some paper and cartridge paper is probably the best. You can buy specially prepared pads with the paper cut to size and mounted either as a book or else as a block, or you can buy sheets and cut them to size. Although cartridge paper is very good to work on it is a little expensive and when you first start it will be wiser and certainly cheaper to use something like typing copy paper. If you have made yourself a clip-board here is another use for it since it can hold your paper firmly for you whilst you sketch. The size of the sheet is a matter for you to decide but you won't want it too large or you will not be able to manage it if there is a breeze; too small will mean that your drawing will be cramped and awkward so choose a size to suit yourself.

You can use any one of a number of drawing materials such as pencils, charcoal, pastel, ink, water colours or spirit colours and you may often want to make use of several together. Charcoal is very popular and has much to recommend it for it can give thick, black lines and thin grey shading; it is very quick and easy to use although it can be a little mucky and a little difficult to clean off if you make any mistakes. If you want to keep any of your charcoal sketches then you will need to 'fix' them which means coating them with a thin layer of varnish or spirit which you can buy at any art shop.

If you prefer to use pencils remember that there are several types, some with hard points and others with soft. A hard point gives a very thin, grey line whilst soft ones leave a thicker black line. The type of lead is shown by a letter on the side – H for hard, B for soft; medium pencils bear the letters HB. Very hard or soft pencils are indicated by a figure as well as the letter, thus 4H is a very hard pencil whilst 2B is fairly soft. You will find that different kinds of pencils can give you different effects and when you go sketching you will probably want to take several kinds along with you.

There are many new kinds of drawing sticks so that you can, if you like, make coloured drawings, however take care for some of these drawing sticks have the colours dissolved in spirit. This means that the colour can go right through the page so that you cannot draw on the back of the paper. Before you use any of the drawing sticks just try them to see if they do soak through.

There are two main approaches to sketching; one is to take a series of quick sketches showing details, size, position and then use these to help you make a complete and careful drawing at home, or you can make a finished sketch straight away. Both methods have advantages but which you use will depend on circumstances.

When all is ready you can then try your first 'field' sketches, that is working out in the open. As you start remember that one of the most important things is to be bold – if you stop and think about every little line before you draw it then you are unlikely to do very much. Look at your subject and then try with bold lines to copy the shape – if it is very bad you can always rub out the line or make a fresh start.

Watch out for perspective – this simply means that you must be sure that the lines of your drawing follow a couple of main rules. If a thing is far away it is smaller than something close and lines which run side by side, parallel lines, seem to meet in the distance. This sounds complicated but if you look at any scene you will soon see that this is what appears to happen.

If you want to check whether two distant objects are the same size or not you can use your hand and pencil as a simple measuring device. Hold your arm straight in front of you and line up one end of the pencil with the edge of the object, now slide your thumb along the pencil until it is level with the other side. If you now keep your thumb in this position on the pencil you can move your arm round and compare this size with any other object.

To give your drawings body and make them look solid you will have to use shading which means that you copy the effect of light and shadow and it is for this job that you will need your various pencils. Soft pencils can give very dark shading whilst the harder ones will give just a light grey effect. Shading is most important for without it your pictures will always look flat and uninteresting.

The best advice to finish up with is 'have a go' and see what you can do – whatever the result you will probably have fun.

Useful Books
Drawing and Sketching, Guy R. Williams. (Museum Press.)
Drawing in Pen and Ink, Faith Jacques. (Studio Vista.)
Sketching in Pencil, Guy R. Williams. (Pitman.)

A Final Word

We have reached the end of our suggestions for your outdoor hobbies and pastimes but there are still many more that we had no room for, looking after pets, skating, football, tennis, cricket, swimming and many others.

You will find some further ideas in another book called *Outdoor Hobbies* by G. Williams which is published by Studio Vista.

If you are interested in these, or any one of dozens more, then why not find out about them by going to the library, asking in school, or writing to the appropriate address given below. Today many of us tend to spend too much of our time watching rather than doing, so make sure that you have some outdoor fun.

Useful Addresses
Camping Club of Great Britain and Ireland.
11, Lower Grosvenor Place, London S.W.1.
Youth Camping Association of Great Britain and Ireland.
38, Elmdale Road, Palmers Green, London N.13.
The Central Council of Physical Recreation.
6, Bedford Square, London W.C.2.

The Scottish Council of Physical Recreation.
  4, Queensferry Street, Edinburgh.
Youth Hostels Association.
  Trevelyan House, St. Albans, Herts.
The Ogwen Cottage Mountain School.
  Bethsada, Bangor, North Wales.
The Boys Brigade.
  Brigade House, Parsons Green, S.W.6.
The Scout Association.
  25, Buckingham Palace Road, S.W.1.
The Girl Guides Association.
  17, Buckingham Palace Road, S.W.1.